Can I sit on your lap while you're pooping?

ACTUAL QUOTES FROM AN ACTUAL TODDLER TO HER ACTUAL FATHER

COMPILED BY MATTHEW CARROLL

ABRAMS IMAGE, NEW YORK

AN EXPLANATION FOR THE EXISTENCE OF *CAN I SIT ON YOUR LAP WHILE YOU'RE POOPING?*

I think I can speak on behalf of parents everywhere in saying that babies are super boring.

But when my daughter, Morgan, stopped being a baby and started talking, things got interesting. Talking is how she tried to figure everything out. And the way I talked back to her was—and still is— very honest and open. I considered it a noble way to engage with a curious child, but, in hindsight, it may have contributed to her early preoccupation with having David Bowie's babies and, also, my imminent death.

As a single dad (or whatever you call a man who spends half his time raising a kid by himself), I had no one nearby to raise my eyebrows at, or whisper "Holy crap did you hear that?" whenever Morgan said something especially weird or bizarrely insightful. Instead, I wrote down the things she said and shared them with family and friends. After a while, it started to feel like this collection of quotes might be valuable, like a portrait or a home movie, so I organized them into this book.

I don't know what kind of woman Morgan will become, but hopefully that woman will one day read the things she said and A) forgive her dad for finding yet another way to embarrass her, B) recognize herself in the crazy, amazing ways she looked at the world when she was just starting to figure it all out, and C) not hook up with super-old David Bowie.

MATTHEW CARROLL
DECEMBER 2014

Play me a harmonica
song about a cat doing a
backfloat.

I'm going to get big
and you will get small
and I will carry you.

Bears bite lions and
lions bite bears.

I'm going to grow up to be a woman, Benjamin will be a man, and Gordon will be a woman.

Some snakes don't bite, did you know that?

It's a good idea to pee in the swimming pool because you can't see it.

I feel quite sick. I think
I am going to throw up
on you.

I'm going to catch a salmon with my arms and eat it all up. I'm going to eat the eyes.

10:57AM | TUESDAY JUNE 9 | 2009

I need to take a break.

I could ride in a wheelchair when I get bigger. I will push it with my arms really fast.

It's OK if you pee in Rachel's backyard.

Cats lick themselves so
they can throw up.

6:54PM | FRIDAY JUNE 19 | 2009

Look at me!

If I had a house with a backyard I would get a really big sloth and keep it there.

6:46AM | SATURDAY JUNE 20 | 2009

Take a picture of
my long tongue!

Get a Father's Day card for me.

Can I sit on your lap
while you're pooping?

We should take the doors off the Jetta because I want to have a Jeep.

It is going to take me a long time to grow up.

I want to drink out
of an udder.

My mother slammed my fingers in the door. You should try that sometime.

Look at me! I'm three
years old! Take a picture!

I'm going to wait right here in this wagon until you push me.

I'm going to ride on your shoulders while you cook dinner.

Let's share. I go first
and you won't get any
until I am done.

Did you ever meet
Smokey the Bear?
He helps children
start fires.

If I am on my bicycle and a deer jumps out of the woods, I will move to the side and not crash into him.

You forgot to give me water! You have to because my mouth is getting very hot.

I don't know how to
say good-bye.

I'm going to eat all your hush puppies. It's OK, they will bring you some more.

If I lean back on
my Big Wheel it is a
recumbent bicycle.

Do you have any hurts on your body? I can put this robot on your hurts and you will feel better.

Yesterday I petted a slug.

How about I eat this key lime pie and you get another pie for you to eat.

I did a big poop just
like you. It's a whole
pile of poop.

Hot tubs are for old people.

Why do you have hair in your nose?

But I want to have diarrhea. Give me more berries!

I want you to make my
hair into an Afro.

This deodorant will make my armpits taste really good.

I'm going to want
your presents.

I checked the computer
and it said you are
dancing wrong.

How do I watch TV on this old toy?

I asked the people at the restaurant and they said no sharing. You will have to get your own food.

I want to go on the space shuttle but I want you to come with me because I think the astronauts might bite.

Take a picture of
me smelling this.

The moon is following us.

I had a dream about a farm. I fed the animals but I didn't pet them.

When I get bigger I'm going to have a baby and bring it to your house. You'll need to get a baby carrier.

Are hash browns nutritious?

Are chicken wings nutritious?

I'm going to play chess
while you poop.

Soon I will be an adult.

It's not too cold for gelato.

I hurt my mind!

It would be really bad
if you had blood all over
your face.

This corn dog is blowing my mind.

You're not my friend and
you're not my dad!

Let's go watch *Bambi* and
you can paint my nails!

It's my job to find candy.

Sliders are hamburgers for toddlers.

If a dog eats peanut butter and its mouth gets stuck and it can't breathe it will die.

I don't want to be an
astronaut anymore.
I want to be a fairy.

This is a lot of ice cream
for a little girl.

If you pick me up
and spin me in the
air we could be in the
Olympics.

Ice-skating would be easier without the ice.

When I'm a fairy I'm going to touch airplanes.

Do you know how to say toenails in Spanish? It's "toenailas."

I think I'm going to
be a vegan fairy.

I want to clean up
the cat vomit!

I'm going to change my name to Cinderella but it's okay if my teachers still call me Morgan.

I would like to have a pet shark, but it would eat us into pieces and then throw us up. So we would have to take baths and then return it.

Could a dragon breathe fire and burn down a whole forest? Well, then could he cook a meatball?

When I'm a fairy I'm going to hunt pigs.

What day is tomorrow? And after that? Then after that? What day is after that? Well, when is it going to be Halloween?

When you die I'm going
to get a new daddy.

It's OK, it's OK.

I'm going to be a fairy rapper because I'm good at rhyming.

You can take a picture
with your eyes. See?
Close your eyes. Now
it's in your mind.

One day could we go to Africa and visit with gorillas in the jungle? I will bring our cat for them to pet.

Is a sandwich a vegetable?

When I'm a fairy I'm going to work on a shrimp boat. Fairies love shrimp.

I can find you a wife.
A Mexican one.

Wait. Are my daycare teachers married?

Fairies like to fart,
you know.

When I am a hundred
I will die, right?

So are these ribs from people?

It's not the end of
the world, you baby.

Have you ever been
to the butt store?

Could we go to Paris and eat snails someday? They kill them, right?

I think our waitress
is from Mexico or
South Boston.

When you're old I'm going to put you in a wheelchair.

I remember things
because I put them
in my mind.

If deer get shot do they bleed? They would have to go to the hospital.

The wind tastes
like candy.

Look at me!

Dumbo's ears are big because he's an African elephant.

I don't know how to
close my eyes.

Hey! Why was my drawing in the trash?

When I am an adult
I'm going to give candy
to children.

I love mystery flavor.

I'm going to name my bunny "Lucifer."

I forgot how to go to sleep.

I'm going to name my giraffe "Lucifer."

Want to know a secret?
My dad likes you.
You should keep your
toothbrush here.

What if you threw up
on the whole world?

I want to have a baby
when I grow up but
who would be the dad?
How do I get him?
What do I say?

Can you sign me
up for church?

I'm going to have two children when I'm an adult. Elliot, a boy, and a girl named Elliouisiouananana.

I just gave my cat
a high five.

When are you going to die?

Tinkerbell doesn't wear a dress. Also she has nipples.

Where do stores get their stuff?

Fairies aren't real but it's fun to use your imagination.

You should be a fairy daddy for Halloween. They wear whatever they want to.

Or wear all black and
you could be my shadow.

I'm a gerbilcorn and this is my house.

If you need a man to
have a baby with maybe
I could get David Bowie.

We should kill an animal and use its blood for paint.

When I grow up I want
to be a stepmother.

Tinkerbell told me she speaks Cantonese.

When I grow up I'm going to have triplets so three babies are going to come out of my vagina.

When I'm an adult can I drive and you ride in the backseat? We can go to a bar.

So they killed the chicken for this sandwich, right? It probably tried to run away back to the farm.

You never know when somebody is going to die.

Princess toothpaste
would taste like skin
and blood.

When I am an adult I will find a man I like and say, "Hello. My name is Morgan. What is yours? Do you want to be my baby's dad?"

When I drank milk out of my mother's nipples it was vanilla flavored.

Can Cinderella and Snow White marry each other?

I'll have my babies
after college.

I would fight Nazis with steak knives.

Maybe you should go to braiding school.

I know how to
draw sausages.

Deer are scared of people so you can't pet them but you could pet a dead deer.